Domo™

UNPLUGGED

By Holly Kowitt
Domo Created by Tsuneo Goda

SCHOLASTIC INC.

New York   Toronto   London   Auckland   Sydney
Mexico City   New Delhi   Hong Kong   Buenos Aires

Who is Domo™

What	Creature
Color	Brown
Texture	Fuzzy
Attire	None
Origin	Unknown
Resides In	Cave
Roommates	Mr. Usaji (a rabbit), Maya and Mario (bats)

Friends	Tashanna (a weasel girl), snake, Bear Boy
Likes	Meat and potato stew
Hates	Apples
First word	"DOMO!"
Second word	"DOMO!"
Only word	"DOMO!"

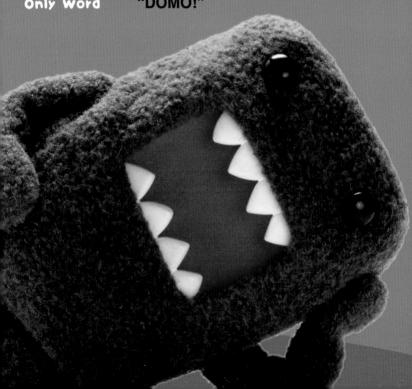

Who is
Mr. Usaji

What	Rabbit
Color	Gray
Profession	Retired
Likes	Green tea, carrots
Hates	Anything meaningless
Wears	Glasses
Description	Old, wise
Quote	"It can't be helped, Domo."

Who is
TaShanna

What	Weasel girl
Color	Yellow
Accent	Weaselly
Likes	Cell phones, computers
Wears	Shoulder bag, one earring
Eats	Apricot and mint tarts
Quote	"I'm the type of girl that can keep a secret . . . ."

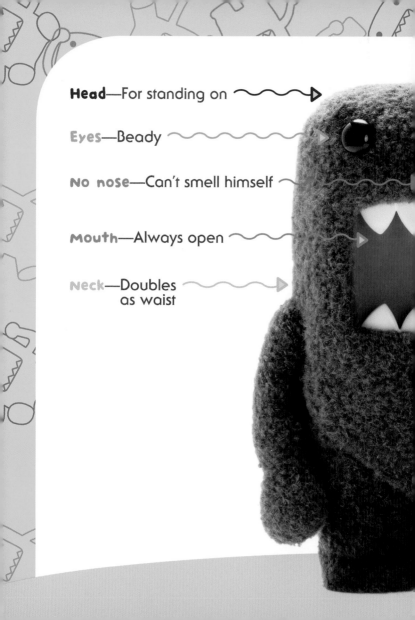

Head—For standing on ～～～▶

Eyes—Beady ～～～▶

No nose—Can't smell himself ～

Mouth—Always open ～～～▶

Neck—Doubles as waist ～～▶

THE ANATOMY OF

Hairstyle—Low maintenance

Heart—Pure

Hands—For playing baseball and the guitar badly

Feet—Shoeless

Domo's
World

Tea	Hot, green, and strong
Rice Bowl	Best food ever
Clock	Time to eat again
Mario	Bat
Baseball Glove	To go with bat
Radio	Music
TV Remote Control	Mine!

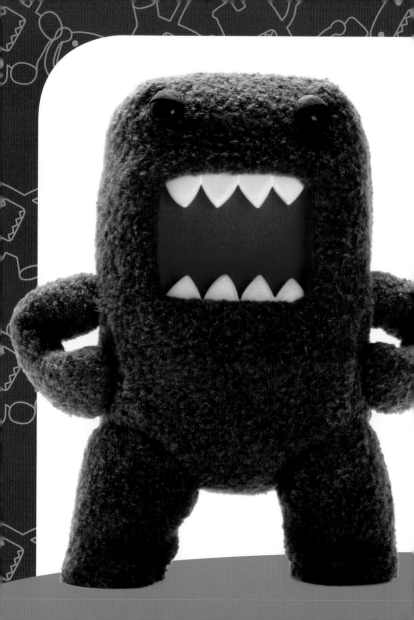

Domo's
TO-DO LIST

 Eat

Check job listings for "Brown Creatures"

Daydream

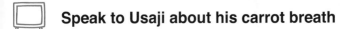 Speak to Usaji about his carrot breath

Watch TV

Eat

Stop at Hole Depot

Domo's
Words to Live By

Don't worry,
be fuzzy.

A hideout is good, but only if it stays hidden.

Don't let life get you brown.

Stand (on your head) for what you believe in.

Think outside the cave.

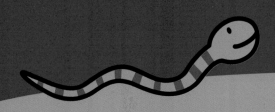

When life gives you
lemons, throw them
at your friends.

Domo to English
Dictionary

"Domo?"	What up, Hungry Bear?
"Domo"...............	No way.
"DOMO!"	Yikes!
"Domo"	Um
"Domodomo"....	As a matter of fact, I haven't had lunch yet.
"DoMO"...............	Darn it.
"Do! Mo!"..........	Uh-oh.
"DOMODOMODOMO!"	Go! Go! Go!
"Domo, domo".	Hee-hee!
"DOOOMOOO" ...	DOOOMOOO!

Five Best Things About Being **Domo**

1. Coffee stains don't show

2. Never need a haircut

3. The dentist never has to say, "Open wide!"

4. Only eight teeth to brush

5. Never have to worry about what to wear!

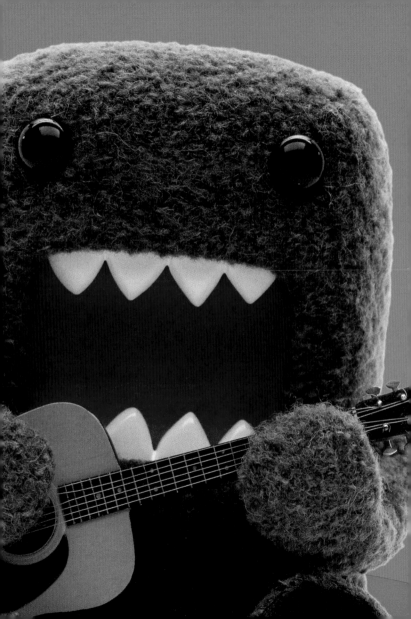

Five Worst Things About Being Domo

1. Necklaces fall off

2. Can't fit through round doors

3. Nothing to wear on laundry day—or ANY day

4. Hard to see tattoos

5. No fingers to scratch your head

A Day In The Life Of
Domo

8 AM	Alarm clock rings.
9 AM	Meat and potato stew. Breakfast is served.
10 AM	Start to put on clothes. Remember you don't have any.

11 AM	Time for work. Fill briefcase with rocks and go.
Noon	Sit at tree stump.
1 PM	Accept invitation to dine with strangely friendly bear. Wonder what's for lunch.
1:15 PM	Narrow escape.
2 PM	Baseball game with woodland friends. Hee and Haw-4. Snakes-0.
3 PM	Go to secret hideout.
3:10 PM	Play with toys, daydream.

3:30 PM	**Friends find hideout, throw party.**
4:00 PM	**Cloud of pink smoke. Party over.**
5:00 PM	**Naptime.**
6:00 PM	**Meat and potato stew.** **Dinner with Mr. Usaji.**
7:00 PM	**Watch TV.**
9:00 PM	**Usaji warns,** **"Never open corner cabinet."**
9:02 PM	**Open corner cabinet.**
9:03 PM	**Hand stuck inside candy jar.**
10:00 PM	**Break jar, confess to Usaji.**
11:00 PM	**Bedtime. Very satisfying day.**

If Domo
Ran the World...

Apples would be labeled "poison."

Brown would be the new black.

Furniture would be indestructible.

Domoween instead of Halloween.

"Big mouth" would be a compliment.

Scientists would study Domo Sapiens.

Top 10 Numbers on Domo's Speed Dial

1. **Tashanna**

2. **Mr. Usaji—no phone!**

3. **Mario and Maya**

4. **Hee and Haw**

5. **Dial-a-Balloon**

6. **Snake**

7. **Meat 'n' Potatoes 2-Go**

8. **Cave #3**

9. **Tree**

10. **Mushroom**

It's **Domo's** World, We Just Live in It

Daydreaming is the best policy.

Loonier
landing.

Domo's

Household
Tips

DST-1

Appliances
Don't forget to plug in the robot dog.

Hospitality
Always put out a welcome bat (either Maya or Mario).

Food
Don't let guests eat you out of house and hole.

Gardening
Remember to water the TV.

Fumigation
Cave must be cleared out twice a week. You know what to do.

Meat and Potato Stew

From: Domo

Ingredients: Meat, potatoes, rice

Directions: Hand Mr. Usaji bowl and wait.

Carrot Surprise

From: Mr. Usaji

Ingredients: Fresh carrots

Directions: Peel carrots, steam carrots, eat carrots. Surprise! As delicious as ever.

Recipe Corner

winter Stew

From: Hungry Bear

Ingredients: Domo, water, vegetables, Mr. Usaji (optional), salt and pepper.

Directions: Put Domo in vegetable pot and stir. Add Usaji only if needed, because most people do not like to find hares in their stew.

1. Always remember
   to say Domo.

2. Curb your robot dog.

3. Be generous. Share loud
   rock music.

4. When entering a room,
   remove head pan.

5. Don't eat
   everything,
   just food.

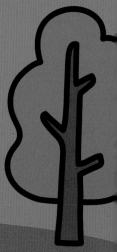

Woodland Gazette

DEAR DOMO: ADVICE TO THE FUR-COVERED

Q. One of my friends has a secret hideout. Do you know who it is?

--Weasel Girl.

A. DOMO!

Q. Our baseball is stuck in a tree. How do we get it out?

--Woodland Friends

A. DOMO!

Q. The candy jar in the corner cabinet is gone. What happened to it?

--Mr. U.

A. DOMO!

Q. I'm cooking a stew of turnips, onions, and meat. What else would taste good in it?

--Hungry Bear

A.

SORRY!
THAT'S ALL
THE QUESTIONS
DOMO HAS
TIME FOR!

--THE EDITOR

Domo's
Book Shelf

Goodnight, Cave

If You Give a
Rabbit a Carrot

On the Night
You Were Hatched

Little Brown
Riding Hood

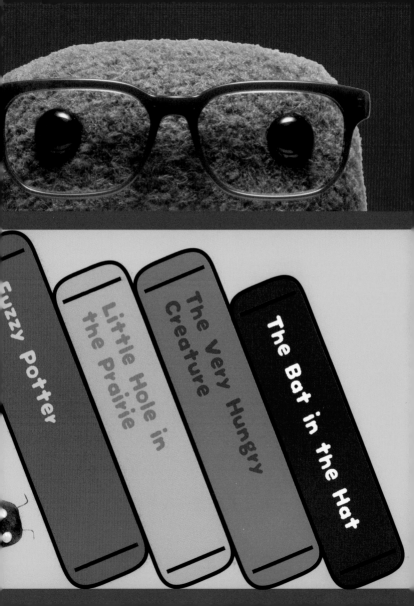

Fuzzy Potter

Little Hole in the Prairie

The Very Hungry Creature

The Bat in the Hat

Domo's
Joke-O-Rama

What did the X-ray of Domo's brain show?
Nothing.

Where do Mario and Maya shop?
Bed, Bat & Beyond

Why did Domo turn right?
The sign said BEAR LEFT.

Why is Domo's mouth like a convenience store?
It's always open.

Why won't Domo join Usaji in a cup of tea?
There's no room!

How did Domo's home decorating book do?
It got cave reviews.

What's brown, furry, and has a trunk?
Domo on vacation.

What part of school does Domo like best?
Show 'n' Smell.

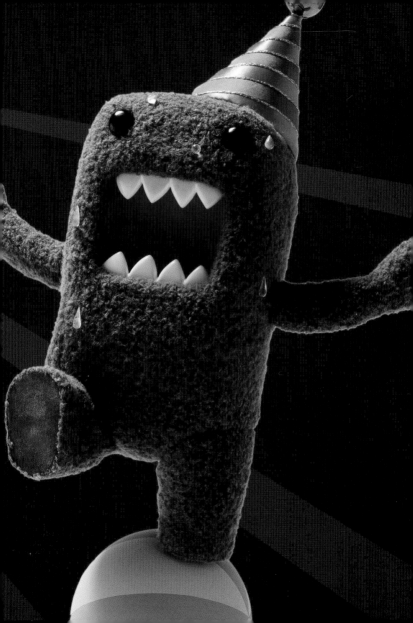

What's brown and goes round and round?
Domo stuck in a revolving door.

What do you call Domo at half-speed?
Slo-mo Domo.

What happens when he speeds up?
No mo slo-mo Domo.

What's Domo's favorite dessert?
Brownies.

How do you make Domo stew?
Turn off the TV.

Why did the bald man put Mr. Usaji on his head?
He needed the hare.

Where does Domo buy groceries?
Hole foods.

How does Hungry Bear like Domo?
With salt and pepper.

What did Maya and Mario say at the end of this book?
Bat's all, folks!

Domo's
Shopping List

Rice

Potatoes

Sticks

Batteries for robot dog

Rocks

Carrots for Mr. Usaji

Air freshener

Domo's
Favorite Bumper Stickers

Honk if you love
Domo

I brake fo
WEASEL.

Hatched to be
WILD

Save the creatures

Have a rice day

Honk *if you love* ~~are~~
Domo

GO BROWN

I ♥ NY

Domo HAPPENS

どーも

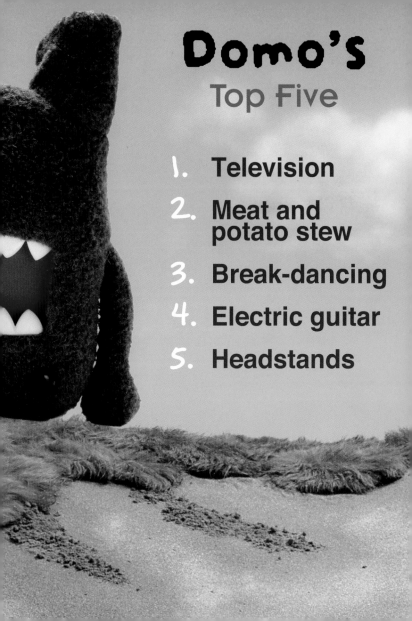

Domo's

Top Five

1. Television
2. Meat and potato stew
3. Break-dancing
4. Electric guitar
5. Headstands

Domo's
Bottom Five

1. **Apples**
2. **Apple sauce**
3. **Apple pie**
4. **Bobbing for apples**
5. **The Big Apple**

More **Domo**
Words to Live By

If you can't play
music well,
play it loud.

Home is where
the rabbit is.

The tea
is always
greener
in the
other
cup.

Weasel come,
weasel go.

Let sleeping robot
dogs lie.

Domo unto others . . .

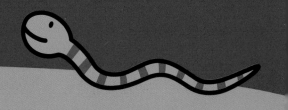

Ten Questions
That Keep Domo
Up at Night

1. Where did I come from?

2. Why do Hee and Haw disappear when Mr. Usaji is around?

3. Why don't I have thumbs?

4. How do you say "Domo" in French?

5. What if it suddenly starts raining apples?

6. What's in the meat and potato broth?

7. Where did my balloon go?

8. Whose giant footprint is that?

9. Where did Mr. Usaji hide the candy jar?

10. I don't cook, so why did Hungry Bear say, "You'd make a great stew"???

The Many Moods
of Domo

Scared

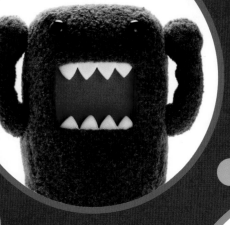

Angry

Sad

Excited

Hungry

Relaxed

Happy

Fuzzy

Domo
The Quiz

1. **Domo comes from**
   a. An egg
   b. A potato
   c. A tree

2. **He lives in**
   a. A pineapple
   b. A cave
   c. A teacup

3. **with**
   a. Two bats and a rabbit
   b. Two bats and a baseball

4. **He wears**
   a. A tuxedo
   b. A bikini
   c. Nothing

5. **He says**
   a. "Domo."
   b. "Domo?"
   c. "DOMO!"
   d. All of the above

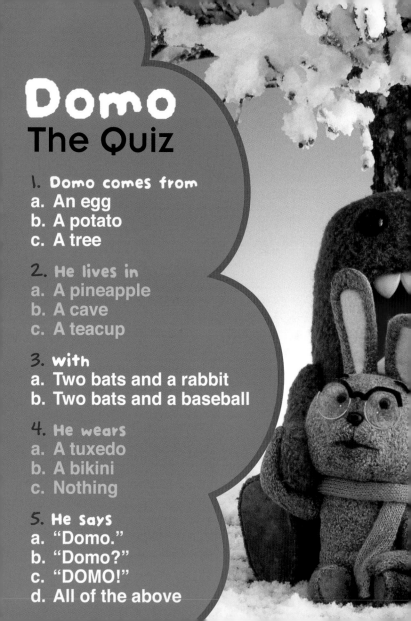

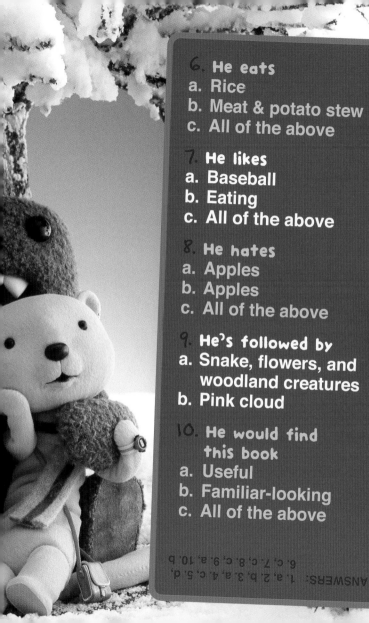

6. **He eats**
a. Rice
b. Meat & potato stew
c. All of the above

7. **He likes**
a. Baseball
b. Eating
c. All of the above

8. **He hates**
a. Apples
b. Apples
c. All of the above

9. **He's followed by**
a. Snake, flowers, and woodland creatures
b. Pink cloud

10. **He would find this book**
a. Useful
b. Familiar-looking
c. All of the above

ANSWERS: 1. a, 2. b, 3. a, 4. c, 5. d, 6. c, 7. c, 8. c, 9. a, 10. b

Who Said It?

1. "You're weird."

2. "Hmmm. Strange."

3. "Whoa, fantastic."

4. "We could use some clothes. I mean, we're all naked."

5. "That is NOT how it's done."

6. "You stepped on my cell phone!"

7. "Wake up, knucklehead. You confuse me."

8. "I'm the winner. I'm the winner. Oh, I love this show!"

9. "But Domo, you just had a meal."

10. "Did anything happen when I was away?"

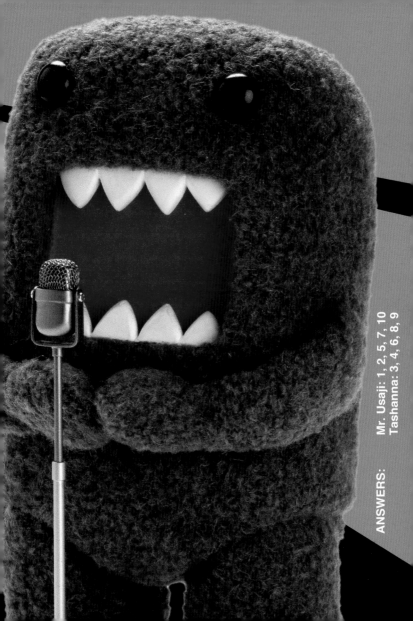

Top 10 Things
Domo
Would Do With
This Book

1. Hide it
2. Throw it
3. Break it
4. Wear it
5. Use it for a paperweight
6. Surf it
7. Bury it
8. Wave away pink cloud with it
9. Read it
10. Sleep on it